DM ME,
MOTHER
DARLING

DM ME,
MOTHER
DARLING

Poems

ALEXA DORAN

BAUHAN PUBLISHING

PETERBOROUGH NEW HAMPSHIRE

2021

ISBN: 978 087233 330 7

Library of Congress Cataloging-in-Publication Data

Names: Doran, Alexa, author.

Title: DM me, Mother Darling : poems / Alexa Doran.

Description: Peterborough, New Hampshire : Bauhan Publishing, 2021. | Summary:
"DM Me, Mother Darling pulses with the confusion, elation, and

shattering fear of 21st century parenthood. Through the eyes of Peter Pan's Mother
Darling and Doran's own experience navigating modern motherhood, the struggles so
often fought in silence come careening forward, electric as the light that defines them.
Through a tangle of casinos, Lizzo, and gravel parking lots, Doran takes readers to a
narcotized Neverland where the mire of grief and the desperation of joy burn with the
same endless flame"-- Provided by publisher.

Identifiers: LCCN 2021004152 (print) | LCCN 2021004153 (ebook) | ISBN 9780872333307
(paperback) | ISBN 9780872333314 (ebook)

Subjects: LCGFT: Poetry.

Classification: LCC PS3604.O725 D58 2021 (print) | LCC PS3604.O725 (ebook) | DDC
811/.6--dc23 LC record available at https://lccn.loc.gov/2021004152. LC ebook record
available at https://lccn.loc.gov/2021004153

For information on the May Sarton New Hampshire Poetry Prize:
http://www.bauhanpublishing.com/may-sarton-prize/

Book design by Sarah Bauhan
Cover design by Henry James

To reach Alexa, go to her website: www.alexadoran.com

BAUHAN
PUBLISHING LLC

PO BOX 117 PETERBOROUGH NEW HAMPSHIRE 03458

603-567-4430

WWW.BAUHANPUBLISHING.COM

Follow us on Facebook and Twitter – @bauhanpub

MANUFACTURED IN THE UNITED STATES OF AMERICA

For Dante,
who may never find Neverland,
but will always find his childhood in these pages.

Mother Darling quivered and went to the window. It was securely fastened. She looked out, and the night was peppered with stars. [...]
A nameless fear clutched at her heart and made her cry, "Oh, how I wish that I wasn't going to a party to-night!"

Even Michael, already half asleep, knew that she was perturbed, and he asked, "Can anything harm us, mother, after the night-lights are lit?" "Nothing, precious," she said; "they are the eyes a mother leaves behind her to guard her children."

She went from bed to bed singing enchantments over them, and little Michael flung his arms round her. "Mother," he cried, "I'm glad of you." They were the last words she was to hear from him for a long time.

—*Peter Pan*, J. M. Barrie

Contents

III. Confession / "I'm an excavator . . . (hey dirt) see you later"

IV. Mother Darling Leaves Father Darling / "A natural void"

Mother Darling Waits by the Window

I ate an orange field
                the day you were born.
Now I drool blossoms and ask the afternoon
to die
        its big death behind me.

I can no longer call it *fenêtre*,
that gap in the aluminum,
where you left me – Oh, Wendy

I wasn't thinking of the winter of it.

Had I understood the humdrum of high alert,
how your gauze blue dress would haunt me

Wendy, what do you see?

Do their eyes guppy when your breath
        hits the shore of the morning sheets?

Do they pluck the burrs from the peach
          oven of your inner knee?

I know now to be a mother
           you must know how to position the shutter.

What angle would have caught
          instead of lost you?

After all,
      I know your brothers will be back.

Little cabbages! Still
        blue with London dirt.

Last night I slipped
into the cigar milk of the same Slainte's pub
I ordered spiked lemonades from
                          when I was your age.

The barmaid says she's seen your face
                        in the shadow of her cobra

      as he strikes his prey.

I.

At the Casino / "Hit me, baby, one more time"

Mother Darling's DMs: 1

Does John know about the tattoos?

The moons that sloop my chest?
   He used to climb those planets
like a necklace, never asking why
     the universe was imploding
   in ink crests, my cleavage
      some lunar wreck.

Mother Darling Talks to God

I know what the other mothers think. I feel their umbrellas against my skin that particular plastic wind they think will skim my conscience. I've already stripped the curtains. Nylon to satin, my house a terrarium, the windows a cloak at my throat. Now, cupcake or semen, they see what I'm eating. They know Father Darling's every stroke. I did not know until now that privacy is a kind of hope – but I don't need a shaft of dust buttered slats or a velvet stuttered draft, I need a home with the eyelids tacked back and a wall wide periscope. And those who suggest this surveillance is a séance do not get that my children aren't dead. No, I don't traffic in magic. My children will fit in the rip left by Jesus when he made that round trip but forgot to teach us how to rise again from the gulches and beaches. Meet me in the bog be hind my house. God, wear whatever you want. Just teach me to see three versions of me, like Jesus saw the Trinity, as the air shaved his body to clove.

Mother Darling's Police Report

Night is the nipple I bruise as I suckle.
My lips burn as they brush star stubble

unsure which constellation to tongue.
Though London calls me the culprit,

that sun-sunk rut was my accomplice.
Yes, this hex is the behest of more than

one goddess but the blame fits like a bodice,
lace tight where it should be honest. *Death,*

where is thy sting? Often, I question what I am
waiting for. A femur? An eyelash to shore?

How much body must they see before
they exonerate me? As if I will ever be

anything but gung-ho guilty. My children
three rings on a tree, an ever-circling inner

grief. At fifty, I have learned nothing is
inevitable as the mangle, some fist always

a-dangle, lush in its yearn to dismantle.
I believed I could Bible in my kin, Jesus

a brushstroke that would paint us in
heaven no matter the sin, but there

was a kink, somewhere I did the wrong
thing – and now the night wins – a long

hallway dormed in visions of goateed
men I once cherry fed just to hear moan

\<after my body was raided\>

I gave birth to a rainbow.
                    A uterus
    slick confection   who now stands mid-tantrum
        fists beating like so many   wings on the window.

: why yes this is the bloom   of all my hopes.
            Basil another avenue if you want to
but Baudelaire believed   we're immensity

come into being   so excuse me if I won't
        let my son   see me as anything
    but a goddess tender-shrunk.   How I churn

the furious nectar of his heart
            like a spoke: every moment has its garland
    when I'm home. And this morning! the wind

tucked against him   arms akimbo
                        Ma, I a bird?
how could I say no   it's hard to explain

that even a word can break   like *mystic*
        which could be the burble
of a cloud   of centuries purpling my mouth

but instead comes out
            as the x-brand soda Mom used to force
                            down *our spouts*
Call it what you want to
                but there is something universal
        about what I've endowed

I finally see how someone could believe
                in B.C. & A.D.
                        so one man could breathe.

Mother Darling Visits the States

It's not that the sky here isn't blue
but that something has to asphyxiate to turn that hue.

I was so sure New England would fit like a skin.

That here in the glacier pucker of Boston
                    I would finally smooth the lumps

left by my children.
I thought God was going to loiter

              around me like an armchair
speak to me in pinstripe *écriture*

   engulf me in mohair. I thought a lot of things
        could happen

if I abandoned London. But even the earth
   has the weight of the sea to bear.

I know it's silly to believe
        New York City is some portal to the holy

that I might recognize Mary the way love
            recognizes heat, that she would not blush

if I asked how it felt to know
                Jesus had to leave.

Mother Darling Goes to the Casino

I can't handle it: the rainbow sop of the slots

the coin clot, the neon scar
    of night that never stops,

 the woman next to me who lets
   fluorescents freckle her hands

   like Jesus let the moon muscle his back
  when everything else was wilderness.

How many of us have asked too much of glitter?
    Have counted on sparkle to bear?

I know that's why my therapist suggested this –
    it's easy to concede defeat

 in the disco-honey of dollars and gin neat.
    She doesn't think I'll ever see Wendy.

   The boys? I ask. *Maybe.* She says for mums like me
    belief is the new baby.

 Coddle it. Nurse it. But, my God, loss has a mouth
    that ferns and ferns. Every morning

its lips un-stitch and I feather its ever-urn.
   The woman to my left places her last bet

 of the night. What will she buy?
Is there a child cozy in some London,

   some quaff of jasmine, awaiting
  the putter of her tokens,

or a husband liquoring away the Sunday
        she wants to use as his grave? Maybe

I am a goddess and
        this is all myth. How else could three children

           just cease to exist? Why else would I be
    in this kaleidoscopic cyst, if not to feel

      the fracture of all I miss
        fed back to me as glitter and hiss?

Some Call It *Bounty*

Before you were born I binge-watched *Hoarders*.
        The hours ample as the antelope
I imagine trampling me whenever
        I forget to dream.   I watched women

wear nothing but yellow as they bricked
themselves in Barbies   little forts of soul
less bodies   loneliness a shade of lip
balm   and a few prize-winning doilies

men who sang suppurating songs to rats
    named *Adolphus* and *Ben*.   Son, I watched and
did not love them.   Saw their weariness wick
and bubble   but did not budge.   I had not yet

layered that champagne glass   with the first chop
        of your sunshine striated locks   or cut
a swath from the cushion   where your head sweat
once bloomed   did not understand that barriers

could be built   by braiding all your residue.
Love is forever a *holding onto*.
        So how come they beseech me to   let go?
(no more umbilical   cord crust mummified

by the bedpost   no more quilt of spit
  up rags   stitched above the bureau) they don't
want to believe love is   obscene. They want
        the pink pattern of moderation.

Lips to ease off lips   breath to exist
        as a poised pant   the perfect counter
        part to the soft parlay   of a kiss.
But, son, I am sloppy   with bliss.   And I

refuse to contain any of it.   So
    let the Florida morning file   across your cheeks
  turn to me   and babble   not words   please
but the moonlight that seeps   through the spokes

    of a bridge   your voice   the uncease   of lunar heat.

C-Section

Sometimes when the room is made of oak

        and I am made of flesh

the room and I mix like air and incense : our fusion a funnel of smoke

That's how you left my body, Buggy

Cloud ladled out of me
        All the other babies

puddling between their mothers' thighs
while you rose like any rainbow

        a fountain of every light / but your own

 Unfettered flume!

the sky spread into a cape around you

*It was better not to touch you
*It was better that the room was white and used
*That the surgeon whispered *trippy* as he felt the willow weight of you

Like all those plump bastards, young and hanging

        from Michelangelo's roof

you were cherub chiseled in the ceiling

and I was artist-peasant-falling
beneath you

Son, to say I was afraid
of the star cough covered in blood/of the birth of my son/of giving gravity
its due

to say that I cannot huff and puff
        enough to keep you afloat

is a version of the truth   that never reaches you   like blades
                      that rotate on a fan

       all you hear is my breath below *choo choo*   *choo choo*

Mother Darling Joins Mums-Meet-Up Online

Two minutes in: an admin claims
                              she's one-fifth Evangelist.
        So I quit.
                  Belief is not a partial business.

  I think that's what I miss most about my kids.
                              They wanted to stampede Jesus.

  Flock is such a soft word
                        for the fang stiff faith
                            of the tiny and zealous.

So why do the other mothers think I deserve this?

Is it because I refuse to share my sadness?
            because I let willows bay

                              the window bouquet and mascara
                  still my cheek each Sunday?

I'd rather agonize to air. I need my grief
                        to hang star-maimed and gaseous

        to drift along the light fixtures
                        to bubble to chandelier

  I so want to believe in this contingent of women

                to swallow them like bees
                      to gorge on their buzz / buck bilious

                          in the honey grip of their rhythm

        but I already know they can't save me
                  can't capture Wendy, Michael, or John

so I log out and let their voices lace in my wake

let their absence hole another
             throat in the honeycomb I've built to shape

   the parts of me words will never taste
             each prism wax and roseate

  as Wendy would be
            pressed against dawn's face.

Kerygma 2: The Aesthetics of Aging

Because it's 1989 Gil squats on the sand razz
    of his exercise mat, lithe and cheery

    in his metallic onesie, telling my mom
        to follow his lead. My mother bops the TV

      when his image goes fizzy, yells *grapevine*
    when the static overrides his plea, pads me

       with gummies so I won't interrupt her
    three-hour Gil-guided routine. Son, I hated

aerobics and every moment she was sweaty
    and happy. The cling of her flamingo pink

shorts and JC Penney perm in cahoots against
    me. I wanted her to know she was ugly.

Now I succumb to the same swine rise,
    have seen you pause to ponder *how*

putrid instead of *how wise* and I want to save
    you from the slather of this greasy light,

from this halo grown too tight, but I'm not
    sure how to help you escape when fate

is shaped so we know our mothers before
    we know ourselves, a spell that won't break.

How to erase the mornings you heard me turn
    to shadow, the bikinis cut too low, the way

    I treated the beach like a Matisse, a pink
       smeared awning made for my body to bow?

"Hit Me, Baby, One More Time"

Pondering life and pop
 & locking to Tupac, pretending
        to blend in with my students
I park the family sedan
          and find myself
      at a strange juncture:
           Does MTV Summer Beach Party still exist?

I mean, can I still catch myself
     in the curl breath
              of Ananda Lewis?
Can I still forest the land
           of tan abdomens and cocaine
                colored sand?

What mother doesn't want
        to sign up for the sand slobber,
           the class
action coochie call
      to Carson Daly,
         to feel the gaudy

        microphone slip
across her thigh?

Waterlogged by the nostalgic
I am the juicy bit
of midlife crisis

    every mother with a StairMaster
     forgot could cry.

Who is to say my son would not feel proud
                to see his mother
  doe along the pier
         a slosh of sunset and gin
              in her wake,
   crisp as a fawn
       caught in the faux horizon?

The Fall of the House of Britney

I am home with the toilet paper and the vodka
and the too pulpy martini.
A glowless fuckery, I am not
what *Bop* wanted me to be.
All that Sun-In wasted on me.
Son, I know Hulk holds the same woe
as '06 Britney did, as the liner notes
to "Toxic," that there's something in
his image that diminishes the PJ cape
that clenches your neck-nape, a pinch
you can't escape. I admit at one point
I saw Britney as something to be
rather than something to grieve.
I wet my hair in Wal-Mart wax
hoping that after-sex sweat was
something I could achieve (thirteen
and a virgin, my prospects were bleak).
When you holler *Hulk Smash*
I feel the power you think comes
with six-pack abs, his green-tinged skin
a macho man's map, but if hurt has
a color it's hologram, that's the only way
we'll grow as flashy as the icons we stan.
And I don't have a recipe or list of glam
accessories that will appease this ugly
need — just a belief that you and I
will rise, another mother-son myth,
while the seraphim skid, unable to grasp
us as we sink into the petal-slick,
our eyes lilac bearded, our toes daisy rich.

Nightsink, Faucet Me a Lullaby

On the nights when my body loves itself
enough to let it sleep

I lower myself into myself and pick a fight
                            with your memory,

never mind that you're asleep right next to me,
                    your curls a comet of sparks spread

soft on the sheets, I'm just that gaga greedy —
but as I click back

through my mind trying to find
                        the nectarine cast of your throat

mid-laugh as I chase you
                    past the lace of shacks and moat

or to the cherry chaw of the morning I met you
            your body a comma behind the Carolina dew,

my mind dives instead to 3:35 on the canopy road
            driving because I need to cry

without facing you, or to the garage where I smoke
                        out the voice of the nursery school

saying you don't fit in with the group.
Eventually I realize

I can't let anything go
not even the bluegold beetles I keep seeing

on the side of the road. I don't know
            if they're dead or just the shed sacs

of bodies now afloat. It's all volcano,
　　　liquid shriek all around me, and I know

　　　　　if I could just soak in the lavender spurt
of the laundry, or lose myself in the apple dream

of the grocery, I could stave off the lava,
　　　keep alive the illusion of in utero. Instead I lie

a liquid berm burning beside your shadow.

II.

OkCupid/ "Blame it on my juice"

Mother Darling's DMs: 2

Does Wendy know you framed her bloodstained panties?

She knows I would never shy
    from the wine-rise a woman feels
      during the pluck of life –
never filter her decanter
  because the public eye can't stand
      her – the rosé maze
of her thighs like a lantern
    I will never turn off.

Mother Darling Joins OkCupid

I never say *mother*, I say *architect*
  I say *body builder, bricklayer of breath*

I say *grief so deep it's just another*
     orifice by which to fuck me

    Interests include: loosening earth's gravity
     waiting for the puck drop,

  and search parties in the nursery.
       I currently define beauty

  as a gin firm face and thighs that speak
     in blitzkrieg. Suitors should be able

  to layer vapor into fog, read the moon
     in my lips, and never mentions kids.

    Dates are just tests, so fill my bubbles
      with your lead, shade the space

  where you believe I should open my legs –
    jog your hand along my labia

    but don't forget – everything made
      in its wake ends up dead.

Mother Darling Flies to Fight Night in Vegas

It no longer feels right to be
    anywhere bodies aren't bursting

to capacity, the sweat-skunk of man
    piss thick upon me. Maybe

I just need to see another man bleed
    to see pain crumple another physique.

    I thought I could glam my way
out of grief, slip like silk

between the gore-gaga celebrities.
    Cocksure as a catwalk kiss

I thought I could panther past
    my memory of boxing-gloved Wendy,

    her ice blue shift adrift between her knees,
her eyes aqua as sky-ripped stream,

    asking me *Do Michael and John feel*
jilted by gender? I mean do boys ever quiver

    under their body's anchor? And so I'm here
to record that quiver, to gauge the tender

of their leather fettered hands, to stencil forever
the tectonics of man on night glossed man.

    What would Wendy think if she were here
among the slink of sweat-gemmed skin?

Would she be convinced men know
    the cocoon burden, that they too spin

their own horizon, or would the lie rise
    between us, another sky sized chasm?

On the Bridge at the Black Bear Exhibit

I ask myself what the fuck I'm really getting out of this. Slaloming my son's stroller down a path shellacked in alligators and purple swamp grass, can I still claim my aim is to educate him? At best, the black bear will be a speck of char buried in the nettle and distance. At worst, she'll be a black bear. Seven feet of curiosity and hunger barreling forth. What is the lesson? Last week in the ocean, my son shot forth, his body an arrow of foam on the waves. I was the only one afraid. Son, am I using the zoo to prime you for the vicious and wild blue of a time when I will just be residue? Is there anything more pathetic than a mother who has pulled her son from the *la la* grip of the playground and plugged him into a scene so Victorian-level creepy that even the stumps that protrude through the creek are acid orange warnings of what lies beneath? When I was eleven I was *light as a feather, stiff as a board*. I believed that magic would eventually come easy, just like maternity, but I can't levitate now any more than I can make my son proud, so if you happen to be a mother who knows the perfect dose to keep your kid afraid, but not necessarily at bay, this is my mayday, or maybe I just need to flick on the TV? Show him the KKK.

My Son Just Started Saying *Mom*

to something beside the sofa
and it is hitting me harder
than the bong rip I took last night.

You know the kind that leaves you
in a limbo, half hazy half max
clarity, and I think this smoky
state fits perfectly, because damn

if he hasn't spent the past ten months
not really knowing me. I was okay
being Lady with the Lavender Scented
Butt Wipes and Lady That Rocks
Against Me in the Night. Those slipped
on like Cinderella's slipper. But now

the stakes have changed – someone's foot
will not configure his fate. How to teach him
to trade shoe size for being kind? To love
regardless – glass or burlap hide? Honestly
it's only a matter of hours before he pins me
for a phony, sees I've signed up for something
I only wish to be.

I don't want to be the one who separates
fairy tale from fact or begs you to let me
meet Whitney or Lindsay or Jack or whoever
is your idea of a living dream at sixteen.

I want to Whitman across the world
with you. Two spouts, no, two fountains,
gushing because the grass, the lobster,
the *alive alive alive*, because the moon-groped
shore is an umbilical cord between us, because
we just started gathering the lilacs and they are
there and there and here.

To My Son, Who Just Heard Me Scream *Fuck*

and turned to me for a hug, I'm sorry I keep confusing
me for the goddess of electricity. Imagine your mama

in charge of the parse of light and dark, lightning bolts
shivering down both arms whenever I want the night

to sputter or the sky to rip apart. To unleash
myself in a vector of heat – son, I am angry

that I am not the sun that reaches your cheeks.
I am f-star furious that I can't blend those binaries,

and yes this is about more than astronomy (although
you have to agree that as a star I would hang

but perfectly), this is about America's hard-on
for atrocity, and your mama's sugar/fire/need

to plug those geysers of white male greed. It's true.
I infringe. I jostle. I say irrevocable things.

All to cage you in. You see, I think I can make you
forget I don't fibrillate the wind. Son, the way

condensation clasps the glass is how I will rise
inevitably to the surface of your life –

not as some womb of weather, snow cocked
like a weapon, but silent as the brine that coats

your tendons, as the grope of muscle to skin.

Motherhood (Exhibit A)

God gave me my anger   as a gift and now
I only want the pity of a martini.

Mothers, we cannot   expect to maintain
our melt. I preach   release   but my dad used

to fold foil   into wands so   I could

fairy   and I still   only believe, but
could never be,   magic.   I know how

to hold   my hit in   while my son searches
the groove in my breast,   burned by a pot

seed when I was 16,   for the just sprigged
parts   of me, for the   blossoms to bunch

to his teeth. The chapped daisies   of my hands
sap his dream.   I say   *this is how you sleep*

I say *dissolve your brain   from your body*
I say *you may not recognize mommy*

on the other side   of reality.
And this is where he giggles   says *it's easy*

as if nothing is   inevitable

as his cheek   giving the moon   a surface to be.

For My Son, Who Asks Me to Replay Lizzo's "Juice"

At three   you have come to love
Lizzo and finally   my legacy
is taking root   At night   when the moon
makes a sailboat of us   all, all

our decks starlit and scarred
   I want to help you   feel the thaw
to teach you   to self-rescue
    using hip hop   using song

    You see   my mom once gifted me
         Cosmopolitan magazine
   and though I did learn   1ˢᵗ step:

pet the perineum   I didn't know
   sex could be anything   but friction
I read each slogan   I tried
         to understand orgasm

    using *Merriam*'s Latin   no one said
just listen to the Jacksons   no one
        ran reggae   along my scars
            let the beat tar

    my throat   Oh son   to let Lizzo
widen your scope
    to let tulips   bastion your fall
   to swelter   in harmony's grope

      is a spell I cast   using uterus
and severed rope   yes music is
  a kind of grass   foot-lush touch
lashed   green ribbons wet with smoke

Mother Darling Wins a Meet and Greet with Jewel

Oh, Jewel, it's not enough to be anti-dream,

I have to fight for the choke of reality,
but your voice makes a mucous

between me and the kids, your lilt
knows the slosh of my soul-skid

so, I thought I could confess to you
where I think they've hid.

This isn't the slur of psilocybin talking,
this is a mother who's hanging

on a hint, who saw a face everyone claims
was moon shard, a tickle in the space glint.

And maybe it's the way Wendy wore
your records thin, or the way you believe

in blonde the way I believe in God, as pure
afterthought, but, Jewel,

what do you think? Could a boy sky-swim?
Convince a nursery full of children

to abandon their kin? and what might Wendy give
in exchange for wings?

Kerygma 3: Notes on Acceleration

I try to explain love using
the Subaru's rearview:

look at what bounces back

but you aren't buttered by the glass
   fractured cast of your ego   so I say

     longevity is one way we test
     for the presence of harmony, but

    the only example that comes to me
    is the condom my stepsister kept

    in her sock drawer, cum curdling
        the ribbed rubber sleeve,

the one we took out sporadically
   to remember the first jism she had

    shepherded into being. But this seems
      . . . obscene to tell a boy going on three

    so I try again   *if love exists on a scale*
     of one to annihilation, consider this

a notch between volcanic breeze and blue
   star leak but burning isn't the action

    I want you to imagine so I offer you
    a sip of tea, peach-cooled, a batch

    that teaches the tongue to rise
    early, and after you swish, gulp,

    breathe, I ask *did you taste it*
but you never answer, the sap a weight,

    a glaze, a sugaring of late snow.

I Am Failing You

Here, you can see it in my hands the
way when air fails smoke it wends ash.
A mother's silence has velocity, wing
speed and at thirty I am still learning
to speak. I say *hurdle* but mean *throat.*
I mean sincerely you can jump right
over me, stun me with dust and I will
still bunny-go. Son, I already have so
many roles. Dust buster, kiss crafter,
forever disciple of my dance teacher
Ms. Trudeau. I know. I know. Morning
becomes a chalice when least expected
so why can't I resurrect into something
you can sip on the go? My mother used
to pause the screen on all the ice skating
queens as they waited for their number
to glow – *you can't fake grace* – there!
Watch her sparkle shot lips fold, her too
big eyes glimpse God, her bun twitch
against the faux snow. What I mean is
climb up on the moss with me. As equals
in this quiver of ether, we can bereave the
mother-child trope. What I mean is melt
into the peat, use your ankles to breathe,
the bog is not a (b)rink for us to glacier
each other's heat – no, it doesn't matter
in what order we grow. Graze your first
taste of champagne, now
                              touch your toes.

"Why I so sad, Mommy?" —Dante, age 4

On the edge of the bed at Electric Beach, I assess the tan no one touches.
Yes, I want your pity. Go on. Goddamn drench me. You see, the secret
is you can make a monster out of anything. The stun of Eve's tongue
among the apple foam, the doily-thick spit spread chin to throat. I think
we forget the alpha green ease of that morning, the whiskey empty
hours always blurring. I refuse to tell my son splendor is a figment of
some garden, that every inch of this abyss tipped earth isn't his for the
larking. Even as his body registers it, I still can't bring myself to say *bad
people exist*. Plum with dawn, I whisper *feel the daffodils press air into wish*, I
take the shore of his finger say *muss pollen into wick*. Son, yours tears prove
everything is a candle if enough light divides the tip.

30 Years Post-Peter, Mother Darling Postcards Father Darling

I thought if coral could exist, so could I.
I thought I could lace below, a shock of
color in water, a shatter of sea-soft spine
but even oceans bury their beautiful & I
am leagues behind where I once thought
I'd rise. I couldn't admit magic wasn't the
culprit – carnage a horizon I refused to
climb. Father Darling, I imagine a glow
in Wendy's kitchen, the snow pulp-soft
as it cries down her thigh. Does it matter
if she's alive or just the blossom-slather
of my mind? Quayside I cave: the sweat
that skunks each sailor mirrors the way I
thought I could exist as sting & drip, a
gloss-thick reminder on your skin. But –
the weight! the three-children-heft, guts
everything. I thought that decade would
hang like a portrait, a fuchsia facsimile
I could rip when the faces no longer fit
but where the sand puckers with tide I
don't hear the gush of gravel I hear
Wendy sigh. You called me a test tube,
a Bunsen burner, built to smoke out
your jr. line, but my burn isn't as blind,
isn't as blue swilled, as you define. I may
have earned an orange that spills, yes,
spills every time, but it isn't as if bodies
come to my light, it isn't as if I sear the
way stars sear night, as if I core the sky.

III.

Confession / "I'm an excavator . . . (hey dirt) see you later"

Mother Darling's DMs: 3

Does Father Darling know you left Confession with a grin?

Eventually night is just
    what runs between the rushes.
Imagine earth's exhaustion
        if it never got to blink
     if it never let the sky swell sable and glint.

Mother Darling Goes to Confession

Father forgive me for I

want to come here fat on God's lower lip, fresh from the edge of its
succulence. I want a mouth to arc my body, something to chart the
treachery, some tongue to carve out a canopy. I want to brag to Him
about the swatch of universe I'm quilted in. *Look, God! I'm cross-stitched in
semen.* It would be a different approach to Him – something besides *God,
you stole my children.* I have theories about a man crawling the void my kids
created, theories about why a virus grows violet shoots before it goes on
hiatus. I don't think lips are meant for sculpting, I don't want to measure
teeth's indent, but something about the bite makes me think a mouth
could resurrect the site that collapsed the night the bay window bucked
and the kids took flight. I want to sparkle with some man's saliva and
brim with his sighs. And, Father? Sometimes I want to change my mind.
Sometimes, I wish the mouth was mine.

The Tallahassee Moms Are Buying Blippi

costumes for their husbands
and I don't exactly hate
bright colors or propeller hats
and, in fact, dig the snap
of suspenders, but it's hard for me
to see the sexy in children's TV

and it could be his bath-of-balls
mastery or his tendency to serenade
the rusty, but is that all it takes
post-pregnancy? a man as posh in pink
as he is suave at Tiddlywinks?

I mean, in some episodes of *Elmo*
Mr. Noodle proves to be . . . bendy
his moustache the thick side of a dream
but this desire is private, not a purchase
and I don't have God, just Whitman,
Father of Sex-Sans-Sin
so I defer to him:
how do I belly this brand of free?

What unlocks the sex-while-mommy key?
The erotic rotted when I entered
maternity: I can't candle a connection
with anyone, can't push satin
against my thigh and sigh
with relief – I have felt whole flocks
take off inside, but now the wings
swell and die, a feather funk that gums
flesh gone numb with time.

I can keep a secret. I can pause
against the pewter nowhere
and beckon with my teeth.
So why the coital chill? the penchant

for PG? What bridge will bring
me to the brink? Will it be painted
in pastel scream à la Blippi? and
how can I tell it won't sink?

Mother Darling Decorates the Christmas Tree

I always did have a thing for Kris Kringle.
                Any man who can shimmy down a chimney

and still be jolly at the bottom
                is certainly worthy in my mind.

                Maybe that's what happened to Wendy.

I keep looking to the sky,
                but she could've gone down the pipes,

arrow set on city life – I know that kind of alive.
                Lately though . . . not to digress

but Father Darling has been celibate
                since the children left, and I'm not sure

where to bury all the energy
                that used to swell our sex.

                O this season of untucking,

of unwrapping, of folds and folds!
                Let me rip through the crepe and uncover

Father Darling's tongue a-slope my toes.
                The tinsel a brittle glitter

in the background as our bodies
                make smoke of the London snow.

How to make a magnet of the night
                to beam my beacon bright

enough to catch my husband's attention
                or even my children? Sometimes I think

I'll find a note. Like under this paper angel's skirt,
            Wendy will have written *Roses: Carolina*

or *Seahorse Smatter on the Sigh of the Horizon,*
    or the boys will have slipped a hint in the wreath for Advent.

I can smell the Styrofoam of the angels

        they made as children, the glitter and the glue,
and the bobble of the haloed heads

            as Father Darling's breath met my mine
                            in the evening's residue.

Mother Darling Smokes a Spliff

Ahhh. The jolt of my gender first – the spurt
        of its outline firm, like the sudden seize

of puberty I swarm to relearn my body,
      to reinvent the prison-plex of my breasts,

           to vogue below the mooncream
     of this London alley until I find

the me who used to dream in doilies,
      who hadn't felt the zippered breath

of Wendy nest below her flesh.
    Let me feel the fake green felt

    of the pool table scrape between my legs,
       the spilled ale spit along my neck,

    a pub-sawed man catch in the flurry
         of my honey and web. Ahh.

Inhale. Watch the cherry crest
      as I smoke out my pre-Wendy self

    melonball all the parts of me
       still stewing in amniotic scent

    and leave me to gorge and gorge
what's left: a marsh of tongues

      I once believed would learn the art
       of luring air into breeze

but now lie dormant, a wet chorus
      ready to be released.

On Metamorphosis

I don't correct my son when he calls
my hash my honey: I want this river

as much as he does, the lagoon spit,
the gloss-on-gloss-off of foam as it

sugars our ship. Mapless, I give him
what you don't have: a life rinsed of

habit. When he asks for the vast &
berried, I plot a winter gorged on

holly. There's so much to gain when
children tell the story. Their snow

ghazals the marble, their voices lift
like barbells – my son screams from

the backseat *I want to button a snow*
boy in blueberries! & we know what

he means: that everything can be
buried, that nature needs a face

not to skew scary. Just beware, son,
nothing is beautiful as a boundary,

& that bouquet we created can end
up a lei, can choke all we made to lace.

Because I Can't Bottle Puberty, I Slip My Son This Seed

son, i am still waiting for someone to accept me at my original potency / to
help me feel oh feel the sprout of this century / as if it were a ladybug neck-
lace / all those wings at my throat / all that tiny ferocity channeled to choke
/ yes someone to deck me in insect weft jewelry (to slur the wing throb into
rope) / so that i never have to tell you i've learned to lick romeo / to feel
the strange seagrass of his lips start to yolk / and it's disappointing the way
everything is disappointing / if you look long enough / but to deter you
from love / just because i got fucked – no – you at least deserve a window /
deserve that curve of clear glow / no wonder they used to tax glass there is
so much to be had / when you know how to look past / son, in a skewer of
winter you will never remember i lived in the light of a young man's couch
/ i mean to say there was snow / i mean to say you will someday know
the same crouch / but rather than burst sidewise / lighthouse barbie / eyes
switched to gorge and spy / you will cease and desist all attempts to hero /
learn the luster of each wave / tame a fountain from the foam

Leaving Lake Ella, I Discuss the Lexicon of Loyalty with My Son

It's not a perfect day but a day you unbuckle and play
monsters by the lakeshore. You teach me to see every tree

as a hand, only differing in degree each reaches
toward me. You touch each branch. And I let August

eat us. Now you have somewhere to be with Daddy.
I say *we can't*. I say *I promise* next time to add *lakeside battle*

to our plans. *Promise?* you squeak, and I realize you aren't
certain what this means. Future probability not on your radar

at three. How to admit not everything I say you should believe?
We pull onto your father's road and I try to sum it up:

no matter what, but trust resists the cut of language and I am
stuck – I grab the heart-weight of your knee and say *feel*

this thumb, its small span, *feel this nail,* its hush – *this is a promise*
the tether of thunder, a rivulet robbed of its run.

When I Ask My Son the Source of His Nightmares

he says *plants* and you know me – so into morphology
I can't help but believe it's the beaucoup de green

that avalanches his peace. Drip drip chlorophyll kiss:
what to align with if not an aster shower, a petunia

flank? What to grip if all the verdant universe bubbles
and aches? You know no one ever draws a womb as

whittled away – which makes me think it's not green
which leaves him afraid, but the husk left in its wake.

There is so much to understand. Like the woman
who trepanned herself for a group of potential fans,

hungry for a hole God didn't plan. Maybe he wants
crimson to outkink banyan, to replace the purr of

verdure, to privilege the red spur of our own sap,
or maybe what breaks him is that the earth is

shamrock bland, perverse in its preference for one
pigment, ivy eyed where once rainbow tanned.

The Neighbors Invite Us to Church

and lest we forget the petrified
look on my face   the downtown
            sprinklers ajazz   all around me, my son
more abuzz than June
                  on the concrete,

let us conjure the fear that freckled my face that day.

How many of us crumple
            as if God were a gust   that could knock us down
                  with an accident   of touch?
            I am not sure

I want my son to see that side of Him

– his feet tucked beneath a pew,
his tongue tucked beneath a hymn –

when right now God is everything.

                                          I still want him
      to feel the thorn glut his forehead   to stitch his skin
nail-numb   to loop his mouth around
                              the language of crucifixion

but at what cost the blazer buried
            prayer   the pulpit plunk resounding
louder than the robin
                  beak drilling song into air?

My son's face puddles   in the fountain's reflection
      a trillion versions of him
                              blend and dreg.
I nod politely and say

I will never be ready to give religion

                circumference

      let God be
a lily pad instead
        a pulse on the water
        a point of departure

              : a green without end

Mother Darling Orders 100 Peacocks

Save me from the stockings   the only thing
          left of the lilt of her leg   a gauze gone
gamless   a skin tone web   which chews
          the atmosphere   of my daughter's bed

Soak up the oxygen   I once reserved
          for my children   fill the pearl pouch
     of the horizon   with your bird clayed breath
I need the cleave of your   vermilion

     to winter the sedge   Ever since Dawkins said
          faith is a form of child abuse   it's all ledge
     even the ottoman is   chubby with regret
          Did I Bible-bloat the kids   Force them

     to gargle God and   never spit Perhaps
they joined some Mary mad sect   Oh, I should
          have made religion   an option not
     a viscous net   You see why I need

     your ancient scream   to vault me nightly
          your feathers to file   the sky
to fragment   the ink   that swallowed my kids
     to reveal which star sucked me   dry

Fuck this thicket I live in   Mince it
          with your million eyes   Shift mosaic
     among my lawn ornaments   I need so
many wings   the nimbus can't numb me this time.

Missive to God

You knew I would buy the disco checked tube top dress and never wear it. You never told me failure could fit like a fentanyl patch or that the club scene was not a twinkle coated Bacardi bath, or that he or he or he would not listen to me when I asked if there was a bathroom to clean up the semen. You didn't have to read my diary or scorch a peephole, at least that's what I'm supposed to believe in. So tell me, God, armed with angels and the dulcet pink pulse of eternal sky, why the invasion? What did you gain when you watched the cemetery dirt turn oak with the sweat soak of our bodies? When he whispered *choke choke* and the gravestones steamed in the snow and I focused on the etching *1909, Vlady*? Or this morning when I cut the mango from my son's throat, the pink yolk of his cheeks, all 22 pounds wilted against me – you waltzed in, sure that just because you put us there that you could stare. But I'm a mother now. The kind who cries because her son went down a slide, and the air and downward glide are a fear she is always breathing. And another thing. I'm the kind of mother who's always leaving.

Flare-Up

I have not thought about death the way you have.
I have a disease that makes me vomit till I die.

Harnessed to the hospital bed, I try to tell my son
why I can't be touched, why so many wires obstruct

what he has come to know as love.
Still. *This,* I think, *is better than Tennessee.*

Better than the Night Deposit gloom
I used to swoon to, better than the boy

who sighed *I'm bored* as I bared
my body, better than the drill of downtown

Clarksville on nights I put reefer aside to feel
the chill of moonshine. For once, I don't

want to learn anything. I try to find a crescent
of skin he can cling to, slit the paper smock,

pretend I'm a robot, say that's why the lights
blink blue. Last week, a pond gathered January

at its lips and we bent over it. The world was
many and we were two. Tonight, you count

the needle-stabbed scabs in my hand but
I can't hear the numbers just the pond lap

the heady swirl of earth losing itself
in an hourless violet splash.

Mother Darling Makes Funeral Arrangements

My in-laws expect me to be sloppy,
     to join the American McDeath party,

grief like a gag on my acuity –
     but surely, I haven't gone this far

just to regale my deceased
     with some flustered undertaker,

boozy with the chance to flummox
     the bereaved. I want to char

the earth with their presence –
     slit the atmosphere like

Wendy's shoulders once slit Venice.
     I want a guest list so concise

we only invite cirrus, wisp
after wisp of daisy-lit sky-drift

parading across three empty urns:
     this is my idea of homage.

No faces purred into place,
     no race to see my guilt

in the shape of cremains.
     We won't be buying burping

caskets or climate-controlled crypts,
     I already wear the blame.

You see, it's bizarre to me you believe
     one day could contain a ceremony

meant to honor three unfinished
   mouths, three unfinished bodies,

ripped so far from my orbit,
   God only permits me to imagine,

    but never to unravel, their pain.

IV.

Mother Darling Leaves Father Darling /
"A natural void"

Mother Darling's DMs: 4

What do we tell our children?

> You must eat loneliness,
> let its acid tines
>   mine your throat.

Mother Darling Leaves Father Darling

Have I been a fool for chandeliers? Yes.
    Have I let light litter our lives? Yes.

    But to blame the solar stain for our mess
        to place all that weight on the luminous

        is to forget how Mozart thickened the night
            the children left, to erase the tinkle

        of my bracelets down your neck
          as we ducked inside that Christmas cozy

    winter fête. Now, in the nursery,
      all the dolls' mouths pouched in dusk,

        each throat a flume untouched, we argue
          over what could save us. We ring

   around-the-rosie Buddha and Jesus,
      buckle under the biblical

    but nothing seems to please us.
      You say I'm fireworks when a lantern

would fit the demand, as if my shine
      could account for your failures as a man

    but there is no degree of UV
      which could obscure a wound

    three kids deep, so what about this
        wattage makes you angry?

      We once puddled the air
      with our progeny, now you poke

at my emptied belly, looking
      for the loose ligature, looking

for the lesion, like my body
      is the only possible reason

for defeat. But I refuse to dim
      anything to save you from some sin

you think will be exposed
      by my nightly light show. Now, hush —

not everything above can crush us.

High Tea

I pour champagne in Batman's cup and think *if Hell's an endless subway system which car will I be in?* Who will save space for the bubbly-laced, the mothers who wine and dine action figures in hopes of never being replaced? My son thinks it's tea, but this is make-believe, so ★poof★ all his superheroes drink 80 proof. A scarlet cemetery of Solo cups between us, make no mistake, this is how we honor Jesus, water to wine just like the Bible teaches. Yet it's not holy I want him to see, but the nightblush of my cheeks, three deep, Etta wilting on a stereo breeze . . . this is what it takes for me to love my body: a goblet of brut berried jazz, speakers moan-soft, rhythm-mad. Yes, I drink. It means I never flinch when a man touches me, means I never shy the licorice thick of my kiss and wince when a man's lips brush these. Isn't that a gift? To show my son what it means to live outside the lines rape lit? To teach him to celebrate his body instead of hate it? Son! I am only brave half sunk in this sapphire wave, but you, heedless of God and His subway crypt, must make my gin-gummed face your compass, must learn each eye an arrow, each breath an exit.

I Give In Again

           to the cartoon gingerbread
     you've nicknamed "numbies"
               the zombie cookies
          that march in mass gluttony
across the screen – what does it mean
          that you know every word to this scene
but wouldn't know Jesus from a drag queen?

At two years old
          I haven't taught you to believe
                              in anything.
The world stretches – the freshest taffy
          sweet for tapping
and I don't want to interrupt mid-chew

to burst in! on all that softness
               to bind that briar to you –
why separate one miracle from the rest?
          The same way you refuse
to see the moon
                    (it's *sun* night or noon)
nothing isn't holy yet
                              in your view.

This morning in the church
          parking lot across the street
we chuck rocks at a tree.
Lean in   I say
          it's part aim, part fate

     and you unlock your elbow
                         a sequin gone liquid
amidst the bricks and stubble
          of steeples
                         so that your rock
wedges into the wounds
               between the roots.

And I am certain this is prayer.

          Our bodies bent in the butterfly clasp
of Florida's air, surrounding
          a pebble, cheering
its small journey
          to anywhere.

Dante watches dolphins die

amongst the faux coral and funnel
of fish eyes that pattern his night
light. Then waits while they resurrect
on the other side; a sort of nautical
parade between now and the afterlife.

He expects them to extinguish

and return. Extinguish and
return. It's not that the painted
blue smiles and comma curved
bodies of these cartoon sea
creatures are Jesus backpacking
between death and life –
but the same interminable spirit is there.

We haven't talked about God

yet we have watched jellyfish
pout against the glass. We have
bought season passes to the butterfly
room. Who knows if they even noticed us?

Their whole world aflutter and my son trying to see
color, and then

seeing color fly.
Magenta lifted its wings and took off.
Violet clung to him.

Still it's not flight that pulls my son
to this circus ring of dolphins,

it's not weightlessness
that dangles like a rope
in a bell to be rung.

How could he choose what to celebrate?

The room glows
we are bent toward each other
two boats in a berth of blue gloom
one-dimensional dolphins saunter by

two by two
two by two

Ode to a Far-Off Dante

Buggy, in the end, you will blame my body.
The bourbon dip of my skin will simmer
into a stew of armpit juice, my torso once
tucked full of you, will fester, its opus of
flab, a sudden wound. I have not bought

the vanity where you will find me chipping
the crust of blood from my pubes or gained
the glossy backfat your friends will stare at
as I stand, a kerfuffle of remotes in hand,
yelling to turn off the cartoons. You are the char

of this fire, my fondant forged in flame,
and I just want to cast my hand along
the spark and gristle of your body
before it bursts, to feel the open shutter
of your mouth as it's shaved from shale to ash,

yes I know, I'm the reason you have to go
through all that. I'm just not sure how to cover
up the bruise my mother left when she undressed,
each stretch mark a violet unscrewed. Buggy.
I don't want to do that to you.

So let's build a curtain for every fetid freckle.
Let's quilt a cover for every tooth. Let's fish
for smoke and vial and vial the dew – anything
to contain me, to gutter the shame taking root.

Mother Darling v. The Grim Reaper

I step into a blossom weary London
 looking for a path to loll on

when a neighbor stops to ask me
 if the children died

with dignity and suddenly petal heavy
 March is the only wreath that fits me.

All the other mothers want closure
to come via party, a garish invitation

 to the cemetery, some silver balloons
 to crotch the breeze while they pat dry

their hors d'oeuvres–shoved cheeks. No.
 I once thought death was our chance

 to be glorious, that dying was designed
 to divine the precious, that ceasing

 to be meant to sift through the bullshit,
 but death is a fog, not a focus,

 it has hands where in life only eyes
 could grope us, it's a strobe

 whose flashes are built to expose us.
 Why cluster around the afterlife

 as if its flame shapes as it decomposes?
 As if melted is the only way

 to get what God owes us? If belief
 is a kind of happiness, then it's the flesh

of my children to which I'm devoted.
  The peach bloom of Wendy in any August,

John and Michael thigh high in crocus:
  This is prayer at its peak –

no dust-dimmed page or grave has this gate,
  so forgive me if it's my progeny

  I seek, not some hearse-horny deity.

Clapping My Crazies Out with Raffi

as we barrel towards Mississippi, I blink past the song
about God & knees, trying to absorb

the orchid aura of the Chevy chafed breeze. I *prefer*
the "Do-Re-Mi," the Julie Andrews woo to Jesus

jarred by a rhyme scheme, but my son loves the way
Raffi makes belugas a melody, so I put my faith

in the interstate scenery, hoping to be saved by signs
for hotlines & scrub trees. Last night my son asked

why I love someone else, *not Daddy*. The answer was
obvious to me but I could see nothing

the cistern of language could brew would bring him
relief. I could not say *this man is a poem*

every inch wrought with intention, every caesura a petal
sinking & your father is a Betty Crocker recipe

gone bland from knead. I could not ask him to recall
the last-minute flights to our car, his dad piss

drunk, *bitch* stuck on his tongue, as we hauled ass to
a drive-thru for ice cream & calm.

We've all turned the knob down on God – better to
hear the bass of some aimless painter

or the gasp of champagne as it tastes air. Perhaps I
gave up the right to ignore prayer

when I brought my son here. This kind of loneliness
spits froth to glass so every sip is castled

in liquid ash & yet I tip my throat, better to catch
the splash. At our exit, I hand my son his drum back,

place his hand so it bears the vibration & ask him
to separate sound from the palm that makes it:

there: in that hover, I say, my love grew tainted.

For My Son Who Asks *Why*

Maybe we only get to be a mother once
   and the rest is repetition   I keep thinking
I'll get another chance at the garden
to glow slick with some stamen   to honey
and honey this womb   Have you seen the
conifer twirled in winter   this is the gentle
with which I would shimmer   if I could
double and brew but   *puff puff pass*   out
is hardly a bedtime story even if the dragon
is delicate not gory   even if the sirens
shed their sex   dredged sweat and invite
you to tarry   who is to say   I deserve two
I never thought of semen   as another kind
of dreaming   but lately it has the same
oracle bright shade   crystal balls emanate
and if I could just gather   in its gloss
muck my ovaries   and toss in its wake then
what   then I could fan out: so many blades

Mother Darling Tends Her Garden

Is it the tomatoes I envy?
    or their ability to stay

red in all this gateless green,
    to hammer the vine with their juices

        while I only leak?
In a patch of yellow stargrass

    I plant Wendy's slip. The cream
rungs rill with dirt and silt.

    And I know earth is made to feather
            souls not clothes, but if hope in all its aloe

could only grow, could nozzle through
            the shamrock and elderberry moat,

I might see something besides the effigy
                of my children slowly

        bloat. After all, every gardener
    is a queen of puncture

a master of *how far how deep*
                the seed should go.

And it's not that I made a mistake or
                even over-aimed, but that I saw

something besides the night as star laced.
            Now all I'm left with is her shape

        her undergarments, her gloves
                and the lobes of white
    stone where her knees
            knuckled a home as she prayed.

On Artillery

It's easy to say this is a path and this is a shore and still be unsure what divides them. So much is a matter of edge. I buy you a drum set. I want you to be loud. Decibels as defense. I watch YouTube drummers: the glimmer of their wrists in the clamor, the shiver of their mallets in the water of their hands. I am making all these plans to keep you buoyant. Adrift on a solar system of rhythm, you, son, will ferry past the tentacles of land. And maybe simple pleasures do exist — but in case I am right, in case it is all caterwaul-cockeye-complexity and every good goddamn moment is clogged with a jillion juicy arteries — then (look there! the chisel of the beat, the bedroom you don't remember, the drumsticks in your fists, the mother I wanted to be) I want you equipped with orchestra pits and drum riffs and anything so soft it slips like a weapon into your hands and drips back out as G-flat.

Because Wikipedia Defines "Cave" as "Natural Void"

I try to tell my son about my purple peacoat and plaid knickers. I think *this* is a song he can hear. I think what if my mother had told me she hated her robes. I think what if we had shred all that silk. She might be able to hear this tune too. I tell him I felt like a pregnant spider – too much pouf, too many extremities. I didn't want to wear that outfit to Miss Skelley's second grade class where I counted her boogers instead of integers, where I was sure to be inured as the gabardine loser. But some questions we can never ask. And when my mother stooped to secure those pompously portioned buttons, I knew the words would never crest my lips the way I wished. There is something to swallow in this. The way my mother swallowed a whole summer at ten, the way there are whole eddies in her I have never skimmed. Son, there is something to mystery, to a dark lick across a purr of sand, but that is not the gift you will get from me. The earth may have purposeful pockets, may be a lattice of voids as natural as God's plan, but I refuse to traffic in the empty, and where I once felt fabric, you will feel hands.

Kerygma 1: We All Fall Down

Fuck,

I watch turtles bathe in your absence.
Breathless and planetary, I forget the sink of things,

forget that at three, you are floating
and I, at thirty, am barnacled at best, am that hooptie

varnish on the side paneling, coating everything
you might otherwise call fresh. Mothers do that.

Cling. Pondside blubbering. Apparently also turtle spying.
On days you're with Dad, I need reptiles, I need

to see the small green wreck of their backs
islanding while I toke marijuana cigarettes

and check my phone to see if you've called yet. Oh,
I am working on a project – don't think it's all

shimmer-on-the-water somber, I know how
to shimmy the stem of my wineglass. But

something about the seesaw yesterday,
the way you couldn't stand Superman

still enough to lift him, keeps rising like resin
in my mind. But it's not bubbling because

of that moment or Superman's godawful
equilibrium but because you listened

when I said *no, this is a breed of gravity.*
Later that evening, seeing your cardboard castle

buckle, you screamed *Gravity! You thief!*
and as the fat silver bricks toppled I knew

we'd lost something more than a makeshift city,
that we'd licked something so heavy

that we will rise forever garbled and tizzied.

Acknowledgments

Thanks to the following journals and an anthology in which some of these poems first appeared (sometimes under a slightly different title):

30 Poets, 30 Poems: "I Am Failing You"
Bayou Magazine: "Motherhood (Exhibit A)"
THE BOILER: "For My Son Who Asks *Why*"
Booth: "Mother Darling Goes to the Casino"
Conduit: "Mother Darling Waits by the Window"
Connotation Press: "To My Son, Who Just Heard Me Scream *Fuck*"
FIVE:2:ONE: "'Hit Me, Baby, One More Time'"
Glass: "Mother Darling Talks to God"
Gravel: "I Give In Again"
Guernica: "Some Call It *Bounty*"
Harvard Review: "Leaving Lake Ella, I Discuss the Lexicon of Loyalty with My Son"
Los Angeles Review: "Mother Darling Flies to Fight Night in Vegas"
Posit: "My Son Just Started Saying *Mom*"
Mom Egg Review: "Dante watches dolphins die"
Mud Season Review: "Mother Darling Decorates the Christmas Tree," "Mother Darling Joins Mums-Meet-Up Online," "Mother Darling Smokes a Spliff," "Mother Darling Visits the States"
New Delta Review: "Mother Darling v. The Grim Reaper"
Passages North: "Because Wikipedia Defines 'Cave' as 'Natural Void'"
Permafrost: "Mother Darling Tends Her Garden"
Petrichor: "Ode to a Far-Off Dante"
Pithead Chapel: "On Artillery"
Posit: "My Son Just Started Saying *Mom*"
Rag Queen Periodical: "C-Section"
Salamander: "The Fall of the House of Britney," "For My Son, Who Asks Me to Re-play Lizzo's 'Juice'"
SWWIM: "Flare-Up"
Tahoma Literary Review: "The Neighbors Invite Us to Church"
VIDA: "High Tea"

The following poems were originally included in my chapbook *Nightsink, Faucet Me a Lullaby*, Bottlecap Press, 2019:

   "<after my body was raided>"
   "Missive to God"
   "Nightsink, Faucet Me a Lullaby"
   "On the Bridge at the Black Bear Exhibit"

Like motherhood, writing a book takes a village. For that reason I am endlessly grateful

to Eleanor Boudreau, who saw fully fleshed humans in the pages of my work, when I could only see ghosts.

to my grandmother, Barbara Gallagher, for supporting me even when I didn't support myself.

to Elias Lopez, who took a chance on me and who gives me life where I once felt only loss. I love you, Daddy Bear.

to Blas Falconer for seeing in me what I could never have seen in myself.

to Barbara Hamby, for believing in me and for teaching me to "be ambitious."

to Alonso Llerena and Dorsey Craft, who took time away from their own brilliant poetry to help with mine.

to Rusty Thornsbery for listening to me sob into so many cups of champagne.

to Nina de Gramont, Barry Kitterman, David Kirby, and Michael White, for years on years of guidance.

to Jude, nothing will ever be the same.

to Jason Bradford. The celebration will never be complete without you. To Shirley, for showing me what a mother could be.

and to my son, Dante, who taught me to love.

The May Sarton New Hampshire Poetry Prize

Lotte Jacobi 1968 (Eus 56)

The May Sarton New Hampshire Poetry Prize is named for May Sarton, the renowned novelist, memoirist, poet, and feminist (1912–1995) who lived for many years in Nelson, New Hampshire, not far from Peterborough, home of William L. Bauhan Publishing. In 1967, she approached Bauhan and asked him to publish her book of poetry, *As Does New Hampshire*. She wrote the collection to celebrate the bicentennial of Nelson, and dedicated it to the residents of the town.

May Sarton was a prolific writer of poetry, novels, and perhaps what she is best known for—nonfiction on growing older (*Recovering: A Journal, Journal of Solitude*, among others). She considered herself a poet first, though, and in honor of that and to celebrate the centenary of her birth in 2012, Sarah Bauhan, who inherited her father's small publishing company, launched the prize. (www.bauhanpublishing.com/may-sarton-prize)

In *The Wreck of Birds*, the first winner of Bauhan Publishing's May Sarton New Hampshire Poetry Prize, Rebecca Givens Rolland embraces an assimilation of internal feeling and thought with circumstances of the natural world and the conflicts and triumphs of our human endeavors. Here, we discover a language that seeks to at once replicate and transcend experiences of loss and disaster, and together with the poet "we hope that such bold fates will not forget us." Even at the speaker's most vulnerable moments, when "Each word we'd spoken / scowls back, mirrored in barrels of wind" these personal poems insist on renewal. With daring honesty and formal skill, *The Wreck of Birds* achieves a revelatory otherness—what Keats called the "soul-making task" of poetry.

—Walter E. Butts, New Hampshire Poet Laureate (2009–2013), and author of *Cathedral of Nervous Horses: New and Selected Poems,* and *Sunday Evening at the Stardust Café*

Rebecca Givens Rolland is a speech-language pathologist and doctoral student at the Harvard Graduate School of Education. Her poetry has previously appeared in journals including *Colorado Review, American Letters & Commentary, Denver Quarterly, Witness, and the Cincinnati Review,* and she is the recipient of the Andrew W. Mellon Fellowship, the Clapp Fellowship from Yale University, an Academy of American Poets Prize, and the Dana Award.

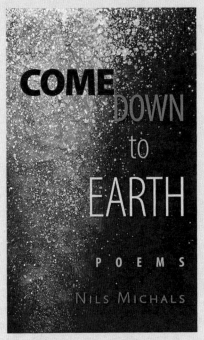

Nils Michals won the second May Sarton New Hampshire Poetry Prize in 2012, and has also written the book *Lure*, which won the Lena-Miles Wever Todd award in 2004. His poetry has been featured in *The Bacon Review, diode, White Whale Review, Bay Poetics, The Laurel Review* and *Sonora Review*. He lives in Santa Cruz, California and teaches at West Valley College.

Nils Michals is alternately healed and wounded by the tension between the timeless machinations of humankind and the modern machinery that lifts us beyond—and plunges us back to—our all-too-human, earthly selves. Supported by minimally narrative, page-oriented forms, his poems transcribe poetry's intangibles—love, loss, hope, a sense of the holy—in a language located somewhere between devotional and raw, but they mourn and celebrate as much of what is surreal in today's news as of what is familiar in the universal mysteries . . . *Come Down to Earth* is a 'long villa with every door thrown open' "

—Alice B. Fogel, New Hampshire Poet Laureate (2014-2019), and author of *Strange Terrain: A Poetry Handbook for The Reluctant Reader* and *Be That Empty*

David Koehn won the third May Sar-
ton New Hampshire Poetry Prize in
2013. His poetry and translations were
previously collected in two chapbooks,
Tunic, (speCt! books 2013) a small col-
lection of some of his translations of
Catullus, and *Coil* (University of Alas-
ka, 1998), winner of the Midnight Sun
Chapbook Contest. He lives with his
family in Pleasanton, California.

David Koehn's first book, *Twine*, never
falters—one strong poem after anoth-
er. This is the work of a mature poet.
His use of detail is not only precise and
evocative; it's transformative."
—JEFF FRIEDMAN, 2013 May Sarton
New Hampshire Poetry Prize judge
and author of *Pretenders*

David Koehn's imagination, rambunctious and abundant, keeps its
footing: a sense of balance like his description of fishing: "Feeling
the weight . . . of the measurement of air." That sense of weight and
air, rhythm and fact, the ethereal and the brutal, animates images
like boxers of the bare-fist era: "Hippo-bellied/And bitter, bulbous
in their bestiary masks." An original and distinctively musical poet.

—ROBERT PINSKY,
United States Poet Laureate, 1997-2000 and author of *Selected
Poems*, among numerous other collections

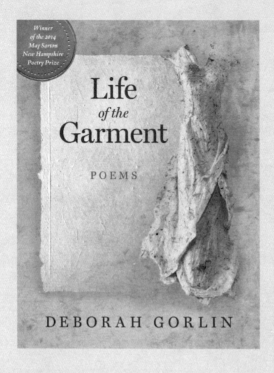

Deborah Gorlin won the 2014 May Sarton New Hampshire Poetry Prize. She has published in *Poetry, Antioch Review, American Poetry Review, Seneca Review, The Massachusetts Review, The Harvard Review, Green Mountains Review, Bomb, Connecticut Review, Women's Review of Books, New England Review,* and *Best Spiritual Writing 2000.* Gorlin also won the 1996 White Pine Poetry Press Prize for her first book of poems, *Bodily Course.* She holds an MFA from the University of California/Irvine. Since 1991, she has taught writing at Hampshire College, where she serves as co-director of the Writing Program. She is currently a poetry editor at *The Massachusetts Review.*

In poem after poem in *Life of the Garment,* Deborah Gorlin clothes us in her fabric of sung words, with characters unique and familiar, and facsimiles of love that open and close their eyes, comfort, and gaze upon us. Read this fine collection—you will see for yourself.

—Gary Margolis, 2014 May Sarton New Hampshire Poetry Prize judge and author of *Raking the Winter Leaves.*

Desirée Alvarez won the 2015 May Sarton New Hampshire Poetry Prize. She is a poet and painter who has received numerous awards for her written and visual work, including the Glenna Luschei Award from *Prairie Schooner*, the Robert D. Richardson Non-Fiction Award from *Denver Quarterly*, and the Willard L. Metcalf Award from the American Academy of Arts and Letters. She has published in *Poetry*, *Boston Review,* and *The Iowa Review*, and received fellowships from Yaddo, Poets House, and New York Foundation for the Arts. Alvarez received her MFA from School of Visual Arts and BA from Wesleyan University. Testing the boundaries of image and language through interdisciplinary work, as a visual poet she exhibits widely and teaches at CUNY, The Juilliard School, and Artists Space.

These poems often shot shivers up my spine. Some made me cry. This is a book I'll want to read over and over.

—Mekeel McBride, 2015 May Sarton New Hampshire Poetry Prize judge and author of *Dog Star Delicatessen: New and Selected Poems*

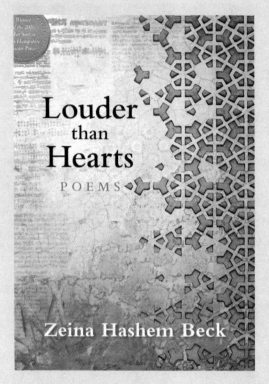

Louder than Hearts

POEMS

Zeina Hashem Beck

Zeina Hashem Beck won the 2016 May Sarton New Hampshire Poetry Prize. *Louder than Hearts* melds English and Arabic, focusing on language throughout.

Beck is a Lebanese poet. Her first collection, *To Live in Autumn*, won the 2013 Backwaters Prize; her chapbook, *3arabi Song* (2016), won the 2016 Rattle Chapbook Prize, and her chapbook, *There Was and How Much There Was* (2016), was a smith|doorstop Laureate's Choice, selected by Carol Ann Duffy. Her work has won Best of the Net, been nominated for the Pushcart Prize, the Forward Prize, and appeared in *Ploughshares*, *Poetry*, and *The Rialto*, among others. She lives in Dubai and performs her poetry both in the Middle East and internationally.

"I don't know how Zeina Hashem Beck is able to do this. Her poems feel like whole worlds. Potent conversations with the self, the soul, the many landscapes of being, and the news that confounds us all— her poems weave two languages into a perfect fabric of presence, with an almost mystical sense of pacing and power."

–Naomi Shihab Nye

Jen Town won the 2017 May Sarton New Hampshire Poetry Prize. *The Light of What Comes After* is an autobiographical mosaic of memory and dreams that speaks to all of us trying to make some semblance of aging and what it means to live well. Jen Town's poetry has appeared in *Mid-American Review, Cimarron Review, Epoch, Third Coast, Lake Effect, Crab Orchard Review, Unsplendid, Bellingham Review,* and others. Born in Dunkirk, New York and growing up in Erie, Pennsylvania, Town went on to earn her MFA in Creative Writing from The Ohio State University in 2008. She lives in Columbus, Ohio, with her wife, Carrie.

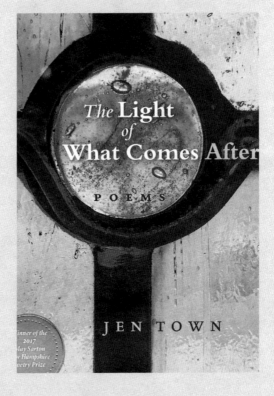

"*The Light of What Comes After* offers a sure manifesto against the domestic and cosmetic. Town's rich linguistic moments and surprising imagery lend her voice a slant which can seem playful and unafraid, but warning is always stitched just below the surface. This is a writer who knows 'Your debts / are more than you'll ever pay back.'"

— Jennifer Militello, 2017 May Sarton New Hampshire Poetry Prize judge and author of *A Camouflage of Specimens and Garments*

MARILEE RICHARDS

The Double Zero

POEMS

Marilee Richards won the 2018 May Sarton New Hampshire Poetry Prize. Richards learned poetry from Charles Entrekin and others after she wandered into a workshop put on by the Berkeley, CA, Poet's Co-op in the eighties while working as an adoption interviewer for Alameda County. Richards attended the workshops for several years prior to the organization dissolving and her move to Arizona in 2001. Her poems have been published in many journals, including *The Yale Review*, *The Southern Review*, *Rattle*, *Poetry Northwest*, *The Journal*, and *The Sun*. She is the author of *A Common Ancestor* (Hip Pocket Press, 2000), and in 2016 she won the William Matthews Poetry Prize.

This is a poet with range—sympathies, anger, tragedy, other people, love, humor. . . . Richards writes unsentimental poems that road-trip through our times and look around at who is with us when we stop to fill up our cars at gas stations, [who] has been with us in offices . . . she reminds us of what the country has gained in consciousness and freedom, . . . what sorrows and suicides we have left necessarily behind, as the bus pulls up at the curb in the don't-you-get-it-yet years we have been motoring through lately.

—David Blair, judge of the 2018 May Sarton New Hampshire
Poetry Prize, and author of *Friends with Dogs* and *Arsonville*

Dorsey Craft is a PhD candidate in poetry at Florida State University. In addition to winning the May Sarton New Hampshire Poetry Prize, she has published her first chapbook, *The Pirate Anne Bonny Dances the Tarantella*, (Cutbank, 2020). Her work has appeared in *Colorado Review*, *Crab Orchard Review*, *Greensboro Review*, *Massachusetts Review*, *Ninth Letter*, *Passages North*, *Poetry Daily*, *Southern Indiana Review*, *Thrush Poetry Journal* and elsewhere. She holds an MFA in poetry from McNeese State University and is the Poetry Editor for *The Southeast Review*.

You will love Dorsey Craft's rollicking persona, pirate Anne Bonny, who serves up heaps of scintillant treasures from the bottomless trunk of her imagination, wit, and verve. In *Plunder*, Jack Sparrow has met his match.

—Deb Gorlin, judge, 2019 May Sarton New Hampshire Poetry Prize, and author of *Life of the Garment*.

In *Plunder* Dorsey Craft creates a ripple in the time-space continuum and brings 17th century pirate Anne Bonny to the 21st century. In these intense and erotic poems Bonny's wild and passionate life finds a place in the heart and mind of a contemporary woman and her struggle for love and freedom. This is a luminous and lyric debut.

—Barbara Hamby, author of *Bird Odyssey*